My name is

● ●

Note to Parents and Teachers

This book is a very first introduction to opposites. It shows
the differences between key descriptions (big, little; wet, dry; fat, thin)
in the clearest and most unambiguous way. It will help young children
to gain a full understanding of this challenging topic.

Oxford University Press, Great Clarendon Street, Oxford OX2 6DP

Oxford is a trade mark of Oxford University Press
Copyright © Oxford University Press 1998
First published 1998
1 3 5 7 9 10 8 6 4 2

A CIP catalogue record for this book is available from the British Library

ISBN 0-19-9104808 (hardback)
ISBN 0-19-9104816 (paperback)

Printed in Hong Kong by OUP Hong Kong

My first book of opposites

Illustrated by Julie Park

Consultant: Peter Patilla

Oxford University Press

tall   **short**

wet   **dry**

slow

fast

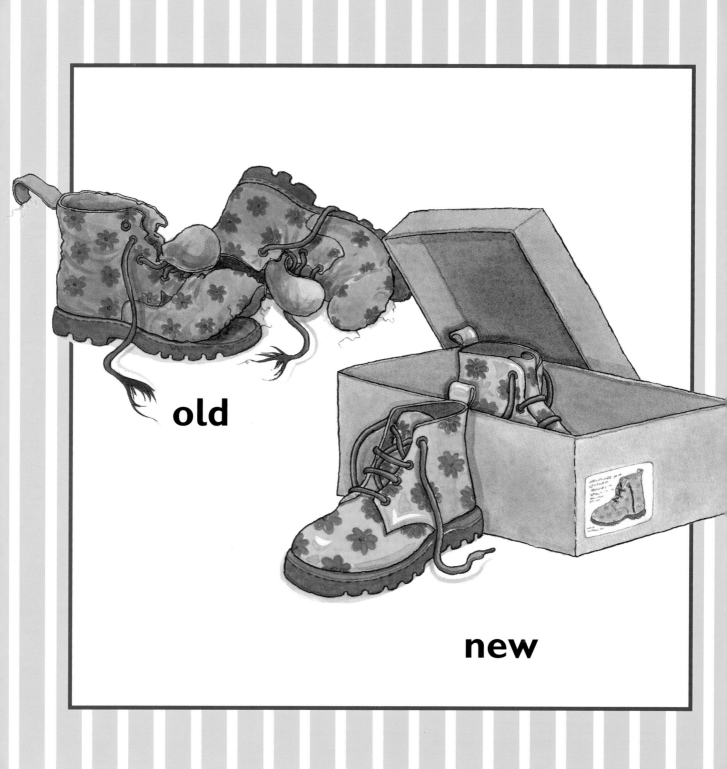

old

new

light　　　　　**heavy**

dark

light

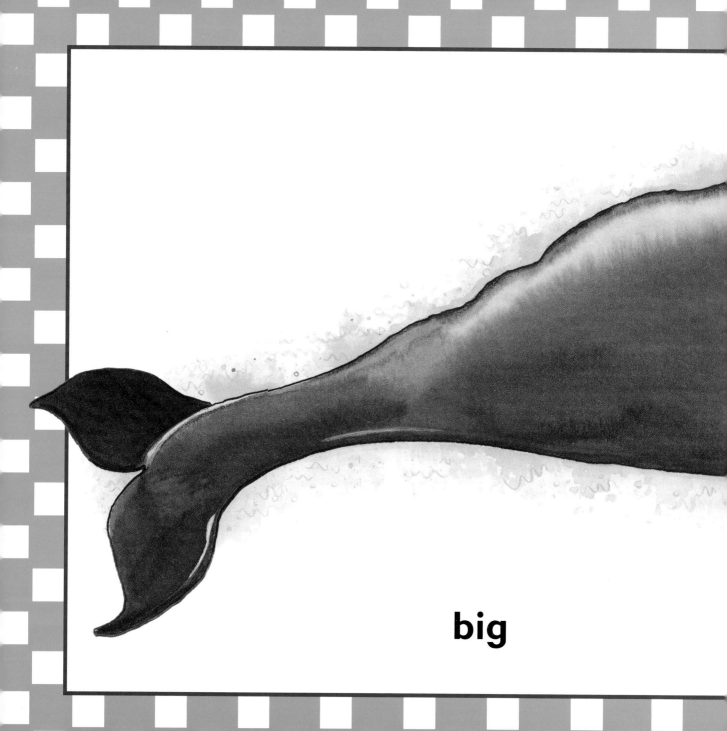

big

little

clean   **dirty**

tight   **loose**

hot

cold

open

closed

happy   **sad**

fat   **thin**

empty

full

good

naughty

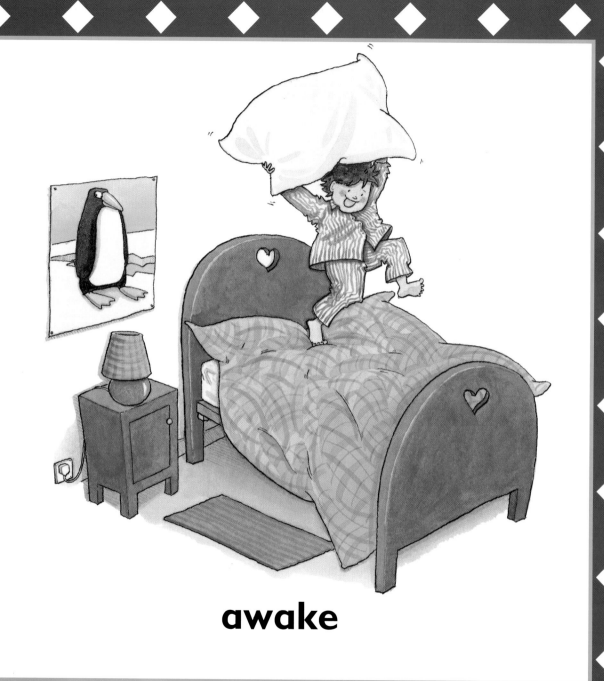

awake

asleep